GW00503379

Contents

Preface

I express my gratitude to God, our Heavenly Father, for bestowing upon me this revelation through Jesus Christ and the guidance of His Holy Spirit. It was within the confines of the Cato Manor Clinic in Durban, South Africa, that I found myself seated on a toilet seat when this divine encounter took place. The year was 2001, and I served as an enrolled nurse, blessed with the privilege of commencing our clinic duties each day with the Word of God and prayer. Prior to embarking on our work, a precious moment was shared among clients and the nursing staff, as we joined together in prayer.

These morning gatherings held great significance, fostering a sense of unity and spiritual connection. I treasured these moments, cherishing the opportunity to partake in prayer alongside those in need of care. My devotion to nursing was accompanied by deep faith, and I was grateful for the chance to infuse my profession with the power of God's Word.

As the dawn of each day graced our clinic, we collectively sought solace in prayer, seeking divine guidance and strength. It was during these intimate moments that the presence of God was palpable, comforting both our patients and the nursing staff. The humble act of gathering in prayer served as a reminder of our shared humanity and the healing power that transcends the realm of medicine.

Truly, it was a remarkable period in my life, where my role as a nurse intertwined seamlessly with my unwavering faith. I remain forever grateful for the grace and opportunity to invoke the presence of God within the walls of the Cato Manor Clinic, offering solace and healing to those who sought our care.

With my Bible always kept close in my drawer, I would seize every available moment to immerse myself in the Word of God. A deep hunger for truth consumed me, propelling me to seek a deeper understanding of His teachings. It was in March of 1987, when I experienced salvation, that I distinctly heard God's voice commanding me to "Run and never look back." In response, I fervently prayed, "Teach me Your Word so that I may run with it. I do not desire to grasp the thoughts of human theology merely; I long for You to be my teacher." Such was my heartfelt plea.

From that pivotal moment on, a relentless hunger for the Word of God ignited within my spirit. I sought to devour its truths and allow its principles to guide my path. Additionally, I yearned for a personal connection with God, desiring to hear His voice speaking directly to me, just as I knew He did with others. Driven by this longing, I embarked on a solitary journey without any external guidance from my pastor or fellow church members.

To create an environment free from distractions, I decided to undertake a three-day dry fast, wholly devoted to drawing closer to God and opening myself to His communication. Recognizing the need for solitude, I approached an elderly woman, a cherished member of the church, and requested to spend those three days of fasting at her home. I humbly asked my husband if he would grant me this opportunity, leaving him with the responsibility of caring for our two sons. My desperation to hear God's voice once again compelled me to take this decisive step.

During those days of fasting, I immersed myself in prayer and sought divine communion. My heart yearned for the touch of His presence and the assurance that He was speaking directly to me. It was a time of intense longing and expectation as I placed my trust in His guidance and eagerly awaited His response.

Packing a few clothes and my work uniforms, I prepared myself for the three-day fasting period, during which I would also be attending to my work responsibilities. As the first day unfolded, my focus shifted entirely towards a single prayer: "Talk to me, please." I was in desperate need of direction, even though I couldn't fully comprehend the reasons behind it. Being a young woman who had recently embraced Christianity but had not yet undergone water baptism or received the Holy Spirit, I felt an urgent longing to hear God's voice once again. The command to "run and not look back" lingered in my mind, leaving me uncertain of its intended meaning. I found myself in a tumultuous marriage, facing such severe challenges that I attempted suicide on three occasions, only to miraculously survive each time. It was after these trials that I found salvation.

However, the circumstances of my marriage left me confused. I questioned whether God's directive to "run" was an instruction to flee from my marital situation. I yearned for clarity, desperate to understand His intentions. Deep within my spirit, I sensed that His message held a different significance, one related to the world at large. I had lived a life of relative righteousness, abstaining from vices such as drinking or smoking, and behaving as a good girl brought up in the church under the guidance of my grandmother. I married at a tender age, with innocence and purity as my companions. I extended help to friends in need, sharing my clothes and meals with them. In my limited understanding, I believed that I had met the qualifications to encounter Him. Yet, I sought further revelation.

As the second day of fasting unfolded, I continued to devote myself to prayer and the study of God's Word, forsaking both food and drink. I hoped such an extreme devotion would capture His attention and elicit a response. However, throughout that day, His voice remained silent, and I did not receive any specific message from Him. Nonetheless, I persisted in my pursuit, fervently seeking a breakthrough and a clearer understanding of His will.

On the third day of my fasting, I experienced an unexpected surge of physical strength. Despite this newfound vigour, I remained disheartened by the absence of a divine message. As the time approached for me to break my fast and return home, I felt a profound sense of discouragement. I dreaded facing my husband without having received a word from God. Uncertainty and doubt filled my mind.

But then, in the very moment when I finished my prayer, His voice resounded within me: "Put off the old man and put on the new man." I was overwhelmed with joy and gratitude. God had spoken to me! It was an incredible moment. Although I didn't fully grasp the meaning behind His words, I rejoiced in the fact that He had personally communicated with me. I knew I had received a word to share with the church, even though I was unsure of its source in the Bible.

Later, I discovered that the verse I had heard was Ephesians 4:22, which states, "That ye put off concerning the former conversation the old man, which is corrupt according to the deceitful lusts." It was a pivotal moment in my journey with Christ. I came to understand that I needed to die with Christ through baptism, allowing my old self to be buried with Him so that I could rise with Him and become a new creation. This revelation aligned with Romans 6:4 in the King James Version: "Therefore we are buried with him by baptism into death: that like as Christ was raised up from the dead by the glory of the Father, even so, we also should walk in newness of life."

With this newfound understanding, my journey with Christ began in earnest. Hallelujah! I was filled with gratitude for the personal encounter I had experienced and the transformative path that lay ahead.

1

THE BEGINNING OF HEARING GOD TALKING

It was the afternoon in the mid-summer in South Africa. The Cato Manor community Clinic was less busy during lunchtime. It would normally be packed in the morning as we had different clients with complex needs. We were providing Primary Health Care, an antenatal clinic, a pediatric clinic, and a geriatric Clinic. I went to the bathroom during my lunch break. As I was standing at the sink, washing my hands, I lifted my hands up and worshipped the King of Kings and the Lord of Lords. I heard the Holy Spirit say, "The way to the Cross." I kept quiet for a few minutes, wondering what the message was all about. The Holy Spirit told me to write a book about this title. He said it is a journey for all believers in Christ Jesus. We need to be prepared to walk and finish the journey. We are the body of Christ, meaning we are joined together in Him and form the glorious body.

When His physical body died, we also experienced a spiritual death with Him. And when He triumphantly rose from the dead, we too were spiritually resurrected with Him. In Romans 6:8 (KJV), it is written, "Now if we died with Christ, we believe that we shall also live with Him." This verse emphasizes the profound connection between our lives and the life of Christ.

Likewise, Colossians 2:6 urges us to maintain our steadfastness in living for Christ, just as we initially received Him as our Lord. We are encouraged to remain deeply rooted and built up in Him, drawing strength from our faith and expressing overflowing gratitude. As believers, we understand that our identity is in Him, and thus whatever happens to Christ, in a spiritual sense, happens to us as well.

This understanding is foundational to the belief that sin no longer defines our lives. Romans 8:1 reassures us that there is no condemnation for those who are united with Christ Jesus. Through Him, the law of the Spirit, which imparts life, has set us free from the law of sin and death. It is through our connection with Christ that we are liberated from the power and consequences of sin.

Lastly, it is acknowledged that Jesus came into this world as the incarnation of the Word of God. This concept is illuminated in the Gospel of John, where it is stated that "In the beginning was the Word, and the Word was with God, and the Word was God" (John 1:1). Jesus Christ, as the Word made flesh, embodies the divine nature and purpose, being the ultimate expression of God's revelation to humanity.

In Luke 1:26 (KJV), it is described that during the sixth month, the angel Gabriel was sent from God to a city in Galilee called

Nazareth. His visit was intended for a virgin who was engaged to a man named Joseph, belonging to the lineage of David. The virgin's name was Mary. When the angel appeared before her, he greeted her, saying, "Hail, thou that art highly favoured, the Lord is with thee: blessed art thou among women." Mary was troubled by the angel's words and wondered about the meaning of such a salutation.

However, the angel reassured her, saying, "Fear not, Mary: for thou hast found favour with God." The angel went on to reveal a remarkable plan: Mary would conceive a child in her womb and give birth to a son. She was to name Him Jesus. The angel further explained that this child would be great and would be known as the Son of the Highest, emphasizing His divine nature and significance.

According to the Word of God conveyed to Mary by the angel, the Lord God would bestow upon Jesus the throne of His Father David. Jesus would reign over the house of Jacob forever, and His kingdom would have no end. This divine message was delivered to Mary, and she accepted it with humility and faith, as depicted in Luke 1:38. Mary, acknowledging herself as the handmaid of the Lord, surrendered herself to the fulfillment of God's Word. Upon her response, the angel departed from her.

By accepting the Word of God, Mary conceived it within her. The Word became flesh through her, as stated in John 1:14 (KJV): "And the Word was made flesh, and dwelt among us, and we beheld His glory, the glory as of the only begotten of the Father, full of grace and truth." The spiritual essence of Christ, as the Spirit and the Word, united with Mary's flesh, forming the physical body known as Jesus. This was necessary for Christ, the Spirit of God, to manifest in human form and walk upon the Earth.

Thus, Jesus came into the world as the embodiment of the Word, born of flesh, and dwelt among humanity. Through Him, the glory of the Father was revealed, and Jesus was full of grace and truth.

Jesus took on human form, becoming flesh, in order to bear the weight of our sins. As sin holds no power over the Spirit, if Jesus had remained solely in His heavenly state as the Spirit, sins would have had no influence over Him and could not have connected to Him. He would have remained untainted by any sin. However, in His mission to save humanity, He willingly took on the nature of sinful flesh, becoming like us.

On the cross, Jesus, in His fleshly form, took upon Himself all our sins. As believers, we are living in the flesh in this world. In order for us to partake in the divine life while on Earth and become joint heirs with Christ, we must experience a spiritual rebirth. As John 4:24 (KJV) states, "God is a Spirit: and they that worship him must worship him in spirit and in truth." Jesus spoke these words to emphasize that to commune with God, who dwells in Heaven, we must be in tune with the Spirit.

Christ, being the anointed one and a Spirit, chose to be born on Earth in human form. He transitioned from Spirit to the flesh. As for us, we must go from flesh to Spirit. This marks the beginning of our journey to the cross. Jesus Christ assumed the form of ordinary humanity in order to fulfil His earthly ministry and accomplish the work of salvation.

Jesus died on the cross and rose again, fulfilling His sacrifice for all human beings. He transitioned from Jesus in the flesh to Christ in the Spirit. After His resurrection, He appeared to His disciples, even though the doors were closed, demonstrating His transformation from flesh to Spirit (John 20:26).

Through His example, Jesus showed us that in order to become new creatures born in the Spirit, the flesh must die completely, not physically. He ascended to Heaven, where there is no flesh, for God is Spirit, angels are spirits, and those who died in Christ are also spiritual beings. Therefore, to engage with the spiritual realm, including dealing with Satan and demons, we need to be in the Spirit.

John 1:12 explains that those who receive and believe in Jesus are given the power to become the sons of God. This new birth is not connected to the flesh, which involves physical conception and the shedding of blood during childbirth. Instead, it is a divine birth initiated by God's mighty hand, drawing people to salvation in Jesus Christ and causing them to be born again through the Spirit of God.

In John 6:44 (KJV), it is stated that no one can come to Jesus unless the Father who sent Him draws them, and He will raise them up on the last day. Jesus Christ came to this world with the purpose of transforming us from flesh to spirit. He, who was originally Spirit, took on flesh to make Himself visible to us. The journey to the Cross begins with birth. Jesus Himself was born of the Virgin Mary in Bethlehem, Judea. His ministry began at the age of 30 and lasted for 3 years, ultimately leading to His death at the age of 33.

Ecclesiastes 3:1 reminds us that everything has its appointed time and purpose under Heaven. There is a time to be born and a time to die. As human beings on Earth, we are initially born through the will of man, through the breaking of water and the flowing of blood. We grow up in the flesh until we reach a certain point where we have the choice to be born again by the Spirit of God. This is a profound transformation. When God draws us to Christ Jesus through salvation, it marks the beginning of our journey to the Cross, where new life and spiritual growth await us.

2

THE PREPARATIONS FOR THE JOURNEY

In John 3:3 (KJV), Jesus answered and said, "Verily, verily, I say unto thee, Except a man be born again, he cannot see the Kingdom of God." Nicodemus, puzzled by this statement, questioned how a person could be born again when they were already old. He wondered if one could enter their mother's womb a second time for a physical rebirth. Nicodemus was referring to the natural birthing process of the flesh, while Jesus was speaking about spiritual rebirth.

Jesus further clarified in John 3:5 (KJV), saying, "Verily, verily, I say unto thee, Except a man be born of water and of the Spirit, he cannot enter into the Kingdom of God." Jesus emphasized that to have communion with God and partake in the heavenly life, we must experience a spiritual rebirth by being born of the Spirit of God. God is Spirit, and everything in the Kingdom of God operates in the realm of the Spirit.

Therefore, Jesus taught that a person must undergo a spiritual birth, born of the Spirit and symbolized by water, in order to enter the Kingdom of God and have a deep connection with Him.

In John 3:6 (KJV), it is written, "That which is born of the flesh is flesh, and that which is born of the Spirit is spirit." Jesus, who originally existed as the Spirit from Heaven, took on human flesh through His birth from the virgin Mary. He willingly became flesh for our sake. As individuals who are in the flesh, we received Him and believe that He is the Son of God from Heaven. Through this belief, we are born again by water, symbolized by baptism, and by the Holy Spirit.

Jesus emphasized that unless a person is born of water and the Spirit, they cannot enter the Kingdom of God. Being born of water refers to the act of baptism, where one immerses in water as a symbol of burying the old self and rising to new life. This new life is prepared to undergo further transformation into the realm of the Spirit when the baptism of the Holy Spirit takes place.

The process of salvation can be likened to being buried and rising again. In order to enter the Kingdom of God, the flesh must be saved through both water baptism and the baptism of the Holy Spirit. Jesus Christ serves as our example, fulfilling these two aspects during His time on Earth. In John 1:14, it is stated that Jesus became flesh and dwelt among us, leading the way for us to follow. Furthermore, in Luke 3:21, we see that Jesus Himself was baptized. As He prayed, the heavens opened, and the Holy Spirit descended upon Him in the form of a dove. A voice from Heaven declared, "You are my beloved Son; with you, I am well pleased." Thus, Jesus was born of water through baptism and born of the Spirit as the Holy Spirit descended upon Him, while the Father's voice affirmed His identity.

In order to have a deep connection and communion with our Heavenly Father, we must be born of both water and the Spirit. This signifies a complete transformation from our fleshly nature to a spiritual one. As we embark on our journey towards the cross, it is essential that we walk not according to the desires of the flesh but in alignment with the leading of the Spirit. This truth is emphasized in Romans 8:1, which assures us that there is no condemnation for those who are in Christ Jesus and walk according to the Spirit, not the flesh.

Furthermore, in Romans 8:35 (KJV), it is revealed that God sent His own Son in the likeness of sinful flesh, condemning sin in the flesh. Jesus willingly took on human form to bear the weight of our sins, freeing us from their power. Sin is rooted in the works of the flesh and holds no sway over the Spirit. Through Jesus' incarnation, He carried our sins, paving the way for our transformation from flesh to Spirit. Let us rejoice in this wonderful truth! Hallelujah!

3

PREPARATION FOR THE WAY TO THE CROSS

C hrist, initially a Spirit dwelling in Heaven, existed in perfect unity with God the Father and the Holy Spirit. However, He chose to take on flesh and be born into this world. He experienced being born of water when John the Baptist baptized Him, signifying a new beginning. Additionally, He underwent a spiritual birth as the Spirit of God descended from Heaven in the form of a dove, affirming His divine nature. Though originally a Spirit, Christ willingly became flesh, demonstrating His incredible love and humility.

To prepare for the journey to the cross, we must:

- Acknowledge our natural birth, which is according to the will of man or the flesh.
- Undergo water baptism, symbolizing a new birth and cleansing.
- Experience the baptism of the Holy Spirit, where the Spirit carries us into a deeper spiritual realm.

- Allow our flesh to be transformed into the Spirit, marking the beginning of our walk.
- Walk in faith, trusting in God's guidance and promises rather than relying solely on what we can see with our physical eyes (2 Corinthians 5:7).

As Jesus approached the culmination of His ministry and the impending sacrifice on the cross, He expressed in His prayer in John 17 that He had existed as a Spirit before coming to earth and was in perfect unity with God. In this prayer, Jesus lifted His eyes to heaven and spoke to the Father, acknowledging that the appointed time had arrived for Him to be glorified. He recognized that the Father had granted Him authority over all flesh, enabling Him to bestow eternal life on those given to Him by the Father. Jesus declared that true eternal life is found in knowing the Father, the one true God, and Jesus Christ, whom the Father had sent. Furthermore, He proclaimed that He had accomplished the work that the Father had entrusted to Him.

In His prayer, Jesus addressed the Father, expressing His desire to be glorified in the presence of the Father with the same glory He had before the world existed. The eternal nature of Christ is affirmed in the opening verses of John's Gospel, where it is stated that the Word, referring to Christ, was present with God and was God Himself. The Word, which was with God from the beginning, played a vital role in the creation of all things. The miraculous conception of Mary resulted in the Word becoming flesh and dwelling among humanity. The unity of the Father, the Word (Christ), and the Holy Spirit is emphasized in 1 John 5:7, highlighting their divine oneness. By discerning the Spirit of God, believers can gain assurance and understanding.

Anyone who acknowledges that Jesus Christ has come in the flesh is from God. Those who are born of God do not habitually sin because God's seed abides in them, and they cannot sin because they are born of God. The transformation from being born of the Spirit involves a shift from flesh to Spirit, and sin holds no power in the realm of the Spirit. This transformation is exemplified by Jesus Christ, who willingly relinquished His divine status and took on the form of a servant, being made in the likeness of humanity. He humbled Himself and obediently faced death, even death on a cross. As Jesus approached His arrest and journey to the Cross, He demonstrated the path we are to follow.

4

JESUS'S PREPARATION FOR HIS JOURNEY TO THE CROSS

The Alabaster Oil: An Act of Spirit-led Worship

In the town of Bethany, at the house of Simon the Leper, a woman approached Jesus carrying an alabaster box filled with precious ointment. With a deep understanding of His impending death and the journey to the cross, she poured the fragrant oil onto His head as He sat at the table.

This woman was granted a divine revelation by God, enabling her to perceive the significance of Jesus' sacrifice. Fueled by the Spirit, she acted swiftly and without hesitation. Unfazed by the opinions of others, even though the room was filled with men, she operated in the realm of the Spirit. For it is only through the Spirit that such boldness and fearlessness can arise.

As believers, we are not given a spirit of fear, but rather a spirit of power, love, and a sound mind, as stated in 2 Timothy 1:7. This woman exemplified the freedom and confidence that come from being led by the Spirit. Her act of anointing Jesus with alabaster oil was an expression of profound worship and obedience to God's revealed plan.

May her example inspire us to walk in the Spirit, unyielding to fear, and guided by the power, love, and sound mind bestowed upon us.

The Disciples' Lack of Revelation

Upon witnessing the woman's act of anointing Jesus with the precious ointment, His disciples were filled with indignation. They questioned the purpose of such apparent extravagance, suggesting that the ointment could have been sold at a high price to benefit the poor.

Despite having constant proximity to Jesus and being recipients of His teachings and miraculous demonstrations, the disciples failed to grasp the profound revelation of His impending death. The revelation of God's plan eluded them, and they remained oblivious to the significance of the woman's act of worship.

Only through the Spirit of God could they have obtained the discernment and understanding required to comprehend the deeper meaning of Jesus' sacrifice. It is by the Spirit that spiritual truths are unveiled and hearts are enlightened.

This incident serves as a reminder that knowledge alone is not sufficient. It is the Holy Spirit who reveals and imparts true revelation, opening our eyes to divine truths beyond our natural understanding.

May this account prompt us to seek the guidance and illumination of the Spirit, so that we may receive and comprehend the profound truths of God's kingdom, rather than relying solely on our limited human understanding.

Unwavering Focus on the Cross

As we journey towards the cross, we may encounter individuals who doubt our vision and attempt to divert our attention away from God's calling. In such moments, we must not lose hope or succumb to fear. Our ultimate goal should be to faithfully fulfil God's will, disregarding the opinions and criticisms of others.

Take inspiration from the woman with the alabaster bottle. She remained undeterred even though men were dining at the table, unconcerned about the possibility of the precious oil contaminating their food. She had received a revelation and seized it without hesitation. Her actions were driven by obedience and determination, and she carried out her task to completion.

In the face of doubt and distractions, we must adopt the same unwavering resolve. We are called to disregard the voices that try to undermine our purpose and stay focused on God's plan. Criticisms may arise, but we should heed the voice of God above all else.

Just as Jesus acknowledged the woman's good work, let us

remember that our devotion to the cross is of utmost importance. The temporal concerns and obligations of this world will always exist, but our time with Jesus is fleeting. The woman's act of anointing Jesus with the ointment held deeper significance as it foreshadowed His burial, symbolizing the imminent hour of His sacrifice on the cross.

As we prepare ourselves for the journey to the cross, let us remain resolute, unswayed by doubt or distractions. May our focus be firmly fixed on fulfilling God's will, knowing that our obedience and dedication to the cross will yield eternal significance. Hallelujah!

5

THE BETRAYAL by Judas Iscariot

I n Matthew 26:14, we read about Judas Iscariot, one of the twelve disciples, who approached the chief priests with a proposal. He asked them, "What will you give me, and I will deliver Him to you?" The chief priests agreed to give him thirty pieces of silver, and from that moment on, Judas sought the opportunity to betray Jesus.

This event marks the second phase of preparation on the way to the cross. While the woman with the alabaster bottle had completed her role by anointing Jesus, Judas emerged as a figure who would fulfill God's purpose in Jesus' life. In our journeys to the cross, we too may encounter individuals like Judas, who play a part in God's overarching plan.

Judas's betrayal serves as a reminder that even amidst acts of faith and devotion, there will always be those who oppose and seek to undermine God's purposes. However, it is crucial to understand that God is ultimately in control, using all circum-stances and individuals to bring about His redemptive plan.

As we navigate our paths towards the cross, we must recognize that the presence of individuals like Judas serves a higher purpose. Their actions may cause us pain and hardship, but we can trust that God's sovereign hand is at work, utilizing even the darkest moments for His glory.

Rather than being discouraged or disheartened by the presence of Judas, we should remain steadfast in our faith and commitment to God's will. Just as Jesus faced betrayal, we too may encounter challenges and opposition along the way. Yet, our faith in God's ultimate victory should strengthen us, knowing that He can turn every trial into a triumph.

In our journey to the cross, let us remember that God's purpose prevails despite the presence of Judas. By trusting in His plan and remaining faithful to Him, we can overcome the obstacles we face and fulfil our calling with unwavering determination. We coexist with others, assisting them and sharing our aspirations. We gather around the table and partake in meals together, yet some of them betray us. It is important to appreciate those who betray us, as they serve a purpose assigned by a higher power. Without Judas Iscariot's betrayal of Jesus, the outcome of Christ's arrival on Earth would have been different. The prophets foretold this event, and it was destined to occur. In Zechariah 11:12–13, it is written, "And I said to them, 'If you think it best, give me my pay; but if not, keep it.' So they paid me thirty pieces of silver. And the Lord said to me, 'Throw it to the potter"—the handsome price at which they valued me! So I took the thirty pieces of silver and threw them to the potter at the house of the Lord." It was part of God's plan. Show love to your Judas Iscariot and entrust them to God. He is the ultimate

Just Judge who knows how to handle Judas. Remember, we must also face our own demise alongside Christ. They are guiding us in the right direction.

6

THE THIRD PREPARATION: THE LAST SUPPER

J esus was explaining the significance of His upcoming death as He sat at the table with His disciples. He even demonstrated it before their eyes, breaking the bread and declaring it to be His body, and lifting the cup and declaring it to be His blood, which would be shed for the remission of sins for the entire world. Jesus emphasized the importance of connecting with Him by partaking in the bread, representing His flesh, and the wine, representing His blood.

By joining ourselves with Jesus, we become members of His body, united in a profound way. Through partaking in His flesh and His blood, we establish a vital connection and share one life with Him. Jesus made it clear that those who do not eat His flesh and drink His blood will not have true life. The Word of God affirms that life resides in the blood. Before Jesus went to the cross, He connected His disciples to His body and His life. They were inseparable from Him, partaking in a deep spiritual union.

As we journey towards the cross with Jesus, our aim is to die with Him, rise with Him, and ultimately be seated with Him at the right hand of the Father. The significance of Jesus' ministry of death was symbolically portrayed on the table during the Last Supper, but the disciples did not fully grasp its true meaning. This revelation can only be understood through the illumination of the Holy Spirit, as hidden truths are revealed by God's Spirit.

As we make our way to the cross, we rely on the body of Christ and His precious blood. His flesh connects us to His body, while His blood connects us to His life and to our Heavenly Father through the Holy Spirit. We are identified as the body of Christ on Earth because our connection to Him is made tangible through the sacred act of Holy Communion.

Matthew 26:17 (KJV): Now on the first day of the Feast of Unleavened Bread, the disciples came to Jesus, saying to Him, "Where do You want us to prepare for You to eat the Passover?" And He said, "Go into the city to a certain man and say to him, 'The Teacher says, "My time is at hand; I will keep the Passover at your house with My disciples." The necessary preparations were made for Jesus to partake in the Last Supper with His disciples before embarking on the journey to the cross.

Matthew 26:21 (KJV): "And as they were eating, He said, Truly, I say to you, one of you will betray Me. And they were exceedingly sorrowful, and each one of them began to ask Him, Lord, is it I?"

And He answered and said, "He who has dipped his hand with Me in the dish, the same shall betray Me." Jesus, being fully aware of what would transpire and who would be the betrayer, possessed divine knowledge. It is God who reveals the hidden things of darkness through His Spirit. Jesus provided them with a sign, yet Judas persisted with his treacherous plan due to his attachment to money. The Word of God, as stated in 1 Timothy 6:10 (KJV), affirms that the love of money is the root of all kinds of evil. Those who covet it have wandered from the faith and inflicted on themselves numerous sorrows.

Jesus had foretold His disciples about the events that would befall Him. He possessed this knowledge even during His time in Heaven as the Christ in the Spirit. God orchestrated and completed everything in the realm of the Spirit before it manifested in the natural or physical realm. Jesus Christ, as the sacrificial Lamb of God, was already slain in Heaven before the foundation of the earth. He came to fulfil what had already been accomplished in Heaven according to God's divine plan.

Matthew 26:26 (KJV): As they were eating, Jesus took bread, blessed it, broke it, and gave it to the disciples, saying, "Take, eat; this is My body." Then He took the cup, gave thanks, and gave it to them, saying, "Drink from it, all of you. For this is My blood of the New Testament, which is shed for many for the remission of sins. But I say to you, I will not drink of this fruit of the vine from now on until that day when I drink it new with you in My Father's Kingdom." After they had sung a hymn, they went out to the Mount of Olives.

This act of partaking in the bread and wine holds great significance in our journey. It represents consuming Jesus' body and blood, providing us with strength, and symbolizing our covenant with our Heavenly Father. It is the blood of the covenant, as mentioned in John 6 verse 51: "I am the bread of life. Your fathers ate the manna in the wilderness and are dead."

"This is the bread that comes down from heaven, so that one may eat of it and not die. I am the living bread that came down from heaven. If anyone eats this bread, he will live forever. And the bread that I will give for the life of the world is my flesh." (John 6 verse 51)

Then Jesus said to them, "Truly, I say to you, unless you eat the flesh of the Son of Man and drink his blood, you have no life in you. Whoever feeds on my flesh and drinks my blood has eternal life, and I will raise him up on the last day. My flesh is true food, and my blood is true drink. Whoever feeds on my flesh and drinks my blood abides in me, and I in him."

If you fail to partake in Jesus' flesh and blood, you will remain disconnected from Him and lack a covenant with the Heavenly Father. Without this vital connection, you cannot complete the journey. It is of utmost importance to abide in Christ and be guided by the Holy Spirit.

In 1 Corinthians 2, verses 10–11, we learn that God reveals His deep truths to us through His Spirit, as the Spirit searches all things, even the profound mysteries of God. Just as a person's spirit knows the depths of their own thoughts, only the Spirit of God truly comprehends the things of God.

In Matthew 26 verse 31, Jesus declares to His disciples that they will all be offended because of Him that very night, fulfilling the prophecy written in Zechariah 13 verse 7. The prophecy foretold the striking of the Shepherd, causing the scattering of the sheep, symbolizing the disciples' temporary dispersal. However, Jesus assures them that after His resurrection, He will go ahead of them and meet them in Galilee.

It is crucial to understand these prophecies and the significance of Jesus' sacrifice. By partaking in His flesh and blood, we establish a profound connection with Him, remaining united and secure in our faith.

Jesus was well aware that once He was taken away, His disciples would lose hope, become afraid, and scatter. This serves as a valuable lesson for us not to rely on human strength alone but to place our trust in God in every aspect of our lives. When we lean on our own understanding, we are bound to stumble and fall. Therefore, it is crucial to keep our focus on Christ throughout this journey—the One who initiated and will perfect our faith—rather than relying solely on human efforts.

Throughout history, we have witnessed many remarkable individuals, both men and women of God, who started their journey strongly. They brought countless people to the kingdom of God, gained recognition, and earned the love and trust of many. However, some of them eventually faltered and fell short of God's grace, causing disappointment for those who had placed their trust in them rather than in God. This serves as a reminder that our ultimate trust should be in God alone, for He is steadfast and unwavering.

During this journey, you may receive prophetic words concerning your life that are yet to be fulfilled. In such times, it is essential not to give up but to diligently pray about them, holding firmly to the word of God and maintaining a steadfast belief that His promises will come to pass. Trust in God's faithfulness and His perfect timing as you continue on this transformative journey.

If a prophecy or vision truly originates from God, it will undoubtedly come to pass in accordance with His perfect timing and season. Jesus, in His remarkable life, fulfilled every prophecy spoken about Him—from His miraculous birth through the virgin Mary, His lineage tracing back to specific bloodlines, the exact city of His birth, His sufferings, His death, and His glorious resurrection. All the prophetic words foretold by the prophets were fulfilled in Him.

In Habakkuk 2, verses 2–3, the Lord instructs us to write down the vision or prophetic words given to us and make them clear so that those who read them may run with them. Although the fulfillment of the vision may take time, we are encouraged to patiently wait for it, for it will surely come to pass without delay. It is important to write down these revelations, pray about them, and patiently await God's appointed time.

Jesus Christ serves as a perfect example of how everything in His life unfolded according to God's precise timing. Just as His life and ministry were orchestrated perfectly, we can trust that God's timing is impeccable in our own lives as well.

7

LOVE YOUR PETER

The importance of God's will cannot be overstated. In Matthew 26:33-34 (KJV), Peter confidently declared to Jesus, "Though all men shall be offended because of thee, yet will I never be offended." However, Jesus prophesied that Peter would deny Him three times before the cock crowed that very night. Along our journey towards fulfilling God's purpose, we encounter individuals who claim to share our vision and promise unwavering support until it is achieved. They offer their assistance in building and praying alongside us. But when difficulties arise, when things go awry, and when challenges emerge, these individuals vanish into thin air. They conveniently forget the promises they made and the commitments they expressed. When questioned about their involvement in our mission, they deny any association, claiming they were merely visitors or had not fully committed themselves. As followers of Christ, let us respond with love and prayers for these individuals. Let us warmly welcome them back if they choose to return when the vision has been accomplished. This is precisely what Jesus did.

At times, God allows "Peters" to enter our lives and deny us, reminding us to place our complete trust in Him alone. This serves as a reminder that our help comes solely from God. He is capable of enabling us to run our race and reach the finish line. It is important to love your "Peter" and pray for their strength and restoration. In Jeremiah 32:17 (KJV), it is written, "Ah Lord God! Behold, thou hast made the heaven and the earth by thy great power and stretched out arm, and there is nothing too hard for thee." Similarly, in Matthew 26:36 (KJV), Jesus led His disciples to a place called Gethsemane and instructed them, "Sit ye here while I go and pray yonder."

In our journey, there are moments that call for separation from the crowd, where we must seek God's presence alone in the upper room. Jesus exemplified this ministry when He departed from His disciples and retreated to the mountain to pray. Isaiah 55:6 (KJV) urges us to seek the Lord while He may be found and call upon Him while He is near. Luke 5:15–16 describes how fame spread about Jesus, drawing great multitudes who sought to hear His Word and be healed from their afflictions. Despite being surrounded by crowds eager for His ministry, Jesus recognized the importance of separating Himself to seek God's face. He understood the need for a fresh anointing and the outpouring of the Holy Spirit. As He took on human flesh, this separation and time in God's presence were vital for His journey to the cross. Similarly, in our own journeys, separation and seeking God's presence can bring great benefit.

In your journey, there are significant blessings that come from seeking God's presence:

1. Fresh revelation: You receive new insights and understanding from God.
2. Strength to overcome the enemy: God empowers you to face and conquer the challenges that arise.
3. The fresh anointing: You are filled with God's Spirit, enabling you to fulfil your purpose.

These powerful tools are crucial for your journey, just as Jesus needed reassurance and strength from the Father as He faced the cross. Regardless of how God might be using you for His glory, it is essential to surrender everything into His hands and seek His face in His presence. Ultimately, it is His work, His glory, and His power. By staying in His presence and listening to His instructions, you will discern whether you are still aligned with His will or following your own desires.

In Matthew 26:37, Jesus took Peter and the two sons of Zebedee with Him and began to feel sorrowful and heavy. During times of trials, tests, tribulations, and temptations in your own journey, not everyone around you may be suitable for sharing your pain. It is important to choose trusted individuals, like your own "Peter" and two companions, who can provide support. Jesus had a specific reason for confiding in only three of His disciples. Although they may not fully understand your situation or offer immediate comfort or intercession, they provide a safe space for you to express your fears, pain, and insecurities honestly. In Matthew 26:38, Jesus tells them, "My soul is exceedingly sorrowful, even to death. Stay here and watch with me."

We have all experienced moments where troubles multiply, everything seems to fall apart, and our faith is shaken. It is an inevitable part of the journey. However, it is in those moments that we witness the powerful hand of God and His miraculous intervention. He lifts us up and turns our trials into testimonies.

8

SUFFERING AND SURRENDER

Wsing a song that reflects the profound truth found in Jeremiah 33:3, KJV: "He lifted me up from the deep miry clay." In times of difficulty, sorrow, and hardship, we witness the glory and grace of God manifesting in our lives. He promises never to leave us or forsake us.

Just as Jesus asked Peter, James, and John to stand with Him in prayer of intercession as the hour of His crucifixion approached, we also need people close to us who can stand in the gap during trials and tribulations. Jesus, fully aware of the unbearable pain awaiting Him, demonstrated the depth of His humanity. He took on the form of flesh, bearing the weight of our sins, our wickedness, transgressions, trespasses, guilt, and evil deeds for the entire world.

Imagine contemplating all the evil under the sun. Jesus willingly embraced our human condition and experienced the same fear and thoughts that we all encounter as flesh. Yet, despite the difficulty He faced, Jesus surrendered His will to the perfect will

Paul, a powerful instrument for spreading the Gospel.

Reflecting on Jesus Christ's journey, we see that His spirit was willing to go to the cross and accomplish the work that God had assigned Him. However, the flesh He took on through Mary was weak due to the burden of our sins. Romans 8:10 tells us, "And if Christ is in you, the body is dead because of sin, but the Spirit is life because of righteousness."

Through Christ's sacrifice and the indwelling of His Spirit, we are given new life and righteousness. It is through His strength that we can overcome our weaknesses and fulfil the purposes God has for us. Let us, therefore, view ourselves and others through God's redemptive lens, focusing on the potential and transformation that can occur when we surrender to His will and allow His Spirit to guide us.

Our flesh, with its weaknesses and limitations, often hinders us from persevering in our journey of faith. That is why it is crucial to listen to the Holy Spirit, who guides us and intercedes on our behalf. Romans 8:27 reminds us that God, who searches our hearts, knows the mind of the Spirit and intercedes for the saints according to God's will. The mind of the Spirit leads us to the will of God.

Jesus acknowledged the weakness of His flesh but demonstrated unwavering obedience to the leading of the Spirit. In His last prayer of intercession before His crucifixion, He said, "Thy will be done, Father." The Spirit led Him to surrender to the perfect will of God. In Matthew 26:42, Jesus went away a second time to pray, expressing His willingness to drink from the cup of suffering, symbolizing the weight of our sins. He yielded to the will of God, even though it meant enduring immense pain.

Perhaps you have experienced moments of prolonged prayer, earnestly seeking God's intervention, only to feel as though He is distant. Eventually, you may have come to the point of surrendering to His will, saying, "If it is Your will, Father, let me carry my cross and continue to follow You." There may have been times when you faced long-lasting problems, causing even your prayer partners to question if you were at fault or had done something to deserve your situation. Some may have given up on you, unable to comprehend why a prayer warrior like yourself could endure such hardships. In this journey, there will be moments when you find yourself alone on the battlefield, facing the schemes of the devil. Even those closest to you, like Peter and the sons of Zebedee, may be found sleeping in their support. But do not give up; continue with the journey.

It is only through the Spirit of God that others can truly understand your situation. People may make assumptions or place blame on you, but the Spirit brings discernment and wisdom to comprehend the complexities of your circumstances. Therefore, rely on the Spirit's guidance, hold onto hope, and keep moving forward, for it is by God's Spirit that you will overcome and find understanding and support on this journey.

You are absolutely right. The flesh often leads us astray and provides inaccurate predictions. Job's story is a powerful example of this. He faced tremendous suffering, and even his friends, who were supposed to stand by him and intercede for him, offered misguided advice and accusations.

In 2 Chronicles 32:8, we are reminded that relying on the arm of flesh, human strength and understanding, is futile. Instead, we are called to lean on the Lord our God, who is our true help and the One who fights our battles.

Jesus experienced moments when He found His disciples sleeping instead of standing with Him in prayer. Even in His darkest hour, when the weight of the world's sins rested upon Him, He went back to pray, repeating the same prayer: "Thy will be done." The task of standing and drinking the cup of suffering was His alone to bear, for the sake of you and me.

On our journey, we will encounter moments when we must take a stand and trust God, our Father. We may face situations where we need to believe that His will has come to pass, even if the circumstances seem contrary. It is in those moments that we must rely on God's strength, wisdom, and guidance, rather than depending on human understanding and our own limited perspective.

Just as Jesus exemplified unwavering faith in God's will, we too can find courage and assurance in surrendering to His plans, even when they are difficult to comprehend. By trusting in God and His perfect will, we can navigate the challenges of our journey with confidence, knowing that He is with us, fighting our battles, and leading us toward His purposes.

10

THE THREE T'S

T he journey of faith involves encountering various tests, trials, and temptations. These three "Ts" are significant aspects of our spiritual growth and development. One notable test is found in the story of Abraham, recorded in Genesis 22:1-2. God called out to Abraham and instructed him to take his son, his only son Isaac, whom he loved, and offer him as a burnt offering on a mountain in the land of Moriah. This was a tremendous test for Abraham, as Isaac was the son of promise. God had previously promised Abraham that through Isaac, his descendants would be called.

Abraham faced the ultimate challenge—to surrender his beloved son, the fulfillment of God's promise, as a sacrifice. It was a test of Abraham's faith and trust in God's character. While it may seem unfathomable and contrary to God's promise, Abraham believed in the faithfulness and truthfulness of God. He demonstrated unwavering obedience and passed the test.

Abraham's example teaches us the importance of trusting in

God's faithfulness, even in the face of difficult and perplexing circumstances. It shows us that God's ways are higher than our ways, and His plans may involve testing our faith to refine and strengthen us. God's instructions may not always align with our human understanding, but as we walk in faith and rely on the guidance of the Holy Spirit, we can discern and follow His leading.

We learn from Abraham's test that God's ultimate plan and purpose surpass our comprehension. He is not a man who lies or changes His mind. His words are powerful and always come to pass. It is through faith, empowered by the Spirit of God, that we can reach the conclusion that God's plans and promises are trustworthy, even when they appear challenging or contradictory.

As we continue our journey of faith, we can draw inspiration from Abraham's unwavering trust and reliance on God. May we approach tests, trials, and temptations with faith, knowing that God's faithfulness will see us through, and His plans will ultimately prevail.

God's purpose in testing Abraham was to assess his obedience and faithfulness. Abraham demonstrated his willingness to obey God's command by taking his son Isaac to the designated mountain. Even in the face of such a challenging request, Abraham declared his trust in God's provision. He spoke words of faith and proclaimed that God Himself would provide a lamb for the burnt offering.

In Proverbs 18:21, we learn about the power of our words.

Abraham's declaration of God's provision aligned with the truth that life and death are in the power of the tongue. Abraham believed and spoke in faith, and his words reflected his trust in God's faithfulness.

Indeed, it was a test, and as Abraham and Isaac went up the mountain, God provided a ram caught in a thicket by its horns as a substitute for Isaac. In Genesis 22:12, the angel of God intervened, instructing Abraham not to harm his son, for God recognized Abraham's fear and reverence for Him. This incident foreshadows the sacrificial love of God the Father, who would ultimately give His only begotten Son, Jesus, to die for the world's sins and reconcile humanity back to Himself.

Abraham's act of obedience and God's provision of the ram illustrate the profound love, grace, and redemptive plan of God. It serves as a precursor to the ultimate sacrifice of Jesus Christ, the Lamb of God, who would be offered as the atonement for our sins.

Abraham's story teaches us the importance of trust, obedience, and the power of our words. Just as God provided for Abraham's needs at that moment, He continues to be our Provider in every aspect of our lives. May we learn from Abraham's example and have faith in God's unwavering faithfulness and provision, ultimately pointing to the ultimate sacrifice of Jesus Christ for our salvation.

Abraham's response to God's provision in his test was marked by faith and trust. He named the place "The Lord Will Provide" as a testimony to God's faithfulness. Similarly, in our own lives, there may be moments when God asks us to do something that seems incredibly difficult or goes against our natural reasoning.

Consider the example of the widow of Zarephath in 1 Kings 17:7−10. She was in the midst of a severe famine, with only enough food left for one final meal for herself and her son. However, when Elijah, sent by God, asked her to provide him with food, she demonstrated faith in God's command. She trusted that if God asked her to give, He would surely provide for her needs.

Knowing who God is and understanding His character and faithfulness can give us the courage to obey, even when it seems counterintuitive or challenging. When God asks us to sacrifice or give up something, it is because He has a second plan, a greater blessing in store for us. Our obedience in the face of testing can lead us to experience God's abundant provision and blessings.

The widow's act of obedience resulted in a miraculous outcome. Despite her lack of resources, Elijah assured her that her barrel of meal would not run out and her jar of oil would not fail until the day the Lord sent rain upon the earth. Through her faith and obedience, God sustained her and her son throughout the duration of the famine.

This story serves as a reminder that our willingness to trust God and follow His instructions, even in the midst of scarcity or uncertainty, opens the door for His miraculous provision. God's ways may not always align with our human understanding, but His plans are always rooted in His goodness and wisdom.

May we learn from the examples of Abraham and the widow of Zarephath, trusting in God's provision and responding in obedience, knowing that He is faithful to sustain us and bless us beyond measure.

11

KNOWLEDGE OF GOD'S WORD

Would you give your utmost, believing in the God of Abraham, Isaac, and Jacob that He will multiply every seed entrusted to His care? On the path to the cross, you will face tests that you must pass. You will find yourself alone in the examination room with only a pen and paper and the invigilator. The teacher and lecturer won't be there to provide answers. Trust in the guidance of the Holy Spirit. Along the journey to the cross, we encounter trials, much like in the story of Job. Despite Satan's attempts to break him down, Job remained steadfast. In Job 1:1–2, we see that there was a day when the sons of God presented themselves before the Lord, and Satan came among them. The Lord asked Satan where he had come from, and Satan answered that he had been roaming the earth. Then the Lord asked Satan if he had considered His servant Job, who was blameless, upright, feared God, and turned away from evil.

To receive such recognition from God Himself is a great honour, as only God is perfect and just. Satan, however, questioned Job's devotion, suggesting that he only feared God for personal gain. Satan pointed out that God had blessed Job's work and increased his possessions, insinuating that Job's faith was dependent on these blessings. This statement by Satan serves as a reminder of the protection and blessings we receive when we trust and fear God on our journey. During the test, it is only you and God as the invigilator, but in trials, it is God and Satan in agreement, with God trusting that you will overcome if you know that your redeemer lives.

On the other hand, Satan eagerly seeks to prove that God is mistaken about you. However, Satan can only touch what God permits. In Job's case, God granted Satan the power to take away everything except Job's life. John 10:10 tells us that the thief comes to steal, kill, and destroy, which is evident in Job's situation. Job 1:20–21 describes how Job responded to his loss by tearing his clothes, shaving his head, and bowing down to worship. Can one truly worship God in such dire circumstances? Yes, it is possible. Job's response was righteous, and he did not blame God. He acknowledged that he came into the world with nothing and would return to it the same way. He recognized that everything he had was a gift from the Lord, and he blessed His name. In similar situations, one might cry out with a voice that shakes mountains, but the most important thing is to worship the Creator of heaven and earth.

Paul and Silas also worshipped in prison, as described in Acts 16:25–28. They prayed and sang hymns to God, and suddenly an earthquake shook the prison, opening the doors and loosening everyone's chains. Despite being beaten and chained, they chose to worship. Why can't we do the same? As 2 Corinthians 4:11

states, we may face death, but life is manifested in others. This is part of the journey. 2 Timothy 1:7 reminds us that God has not given us a spirit of fear but of power, love, and a sound mind. So, do not be ashamed of testifying for the Lord or sharing in the sufferings for the sake of the gospel, relying on God's power.

Satan failed to lead Job into sin, so he returned with a different strategy. Along our journey to the cross, we will all face various trials and challenges. If Satan is defeated and his plans fail, he will resort to attacking our flesh. It is crucial to crucify the flesh and resist the devil, who will then flee from us. We should live according to the Spirit of God, as the flesh is weak, but the Spirit is willing. This transformation from flesh to Spirit enables us to withstand the devil's arrows. In Job 2:4, Satan once again approached the Lord and suggested that Job would curse Him if he were afflicted physically. With God's permission, Satan afflicted Job with painful boils from head to toe.

Ironically, the one who was supposed to support Job through these trials, his wife, instead urged him to curse God and die. She aligned with Satan's desires, entering through his wife just as he did in the Garden of Eden. However, Job remained faithful to God and maintained his integrity. He responded to his wife's words by saying, "You speak as one of the foolish women speaks. Shall we receive good from God, and shall we not receive evil?" Job did not sin with his lips; he chose to guard his words during the trial. As Psalm 19:14 affirms, may the words of our mouths and the meditations of our hearts be pleasing in God's sight, for He is our strength and redeemer.

When Job's trial came to an end, God restored everything he had lost, multiplying it a hundredfold. However, when Job's friends arrived, they stayed silent for seven days, but their subsequent words turned negative. They wrongly perceived Job's situation, judging him based on their limited understanding, assuming he and his family had sinned against God. On this journey, family, friends, and relatives may distance themselves due to the challenges we face. However, we must not lose hope but instead, trust in God's faithfulness. As Joel 2:25 promises, God will restore the years that the locusts have eaten. The end of difficult trials leads to restoration.

Temptation is a battlefield where it is just you and the devil. God does not send the devil; he acts on his own accord. Luke 4:1–13 recounts Jesus' temptation in the wilderness. Led by the Holy Spirit, Jesus endured forty days of temptation by the devil. Although physically weak from fasting, Jesus fought back with the Word of God. Satan attempted to twist Scripture, but Jesus, being the Word made flesh, could not be deceived. Jesus resisted Satan's temptations and proclaimed that only the Lord should be worshipped and served. After exhausting all his temptations, Satan left Jesus for a season.

Jesus' example teaches us the importance of knowing the Word of God and understanding our identity in Christ. Satan will continue to use various tactics against us, as he did with Jesus. He may distort the Word, appeal to our desires, or attempt to lead us into presumption. However, we must stand firm and fight back with the truth. These are the three Ts we encounter on our journey: tests, trials, and temptations. To withstand them, we must be filled with the Holy Spirit and saturated in God's Word, just like a sponge soaked in water. When the devil touches us, the Word of God should flow out of us.

12

FAITH AND OBEDIENCE

Giving the last and best that we have to God and trusting in His multiplication is an act of faith and obedience. As we journey towards the cross, we will undoubtedly face tests and trials that will challenge our faith. In those moments, it is essential to ensure that we pass our tests, for we will find ourselves alone in the examination room, with only ourselves, a pen, paper, and the invigilator.

Just as a teacher or lecturer may not be present to provide us with answers during an exam, we must rely on the Holy Spirit for guidance and wisdom. He is our Helper and Teacher, leading us into all truth and providing the understanding we need to navigate the trials we encounter.

The story of Job serves as a powerful example of enduring trials. Satan sought to break Job down and test his faith in various ways, but he ultimately failed. In Job 1:1–2, we see that Satan came among the sons of God as they presented themselves before the Lord. God, knowing the integrity of Job, asked Satan if he had considered Job, describing him as a perfect and upright man who feared God and turned away from evil.

Job's journey through intense suffering reveals his steadfastness and trust in God. Despite losing his possessions, his children, and even his health, Job remained faithful. His friends questioned him, and he experienced immense emotional and physical anguish. Yet, through it all, he held onto his faith and trust in God, refusing to curse Him.

Job's story teaches us the importance of maintaining our faith and trust in God, even in the midst of trials. It reminds us that the enemy may seek to test and break us, but with God on our side, we can stand firm. God's ultimate purpose for Job's testing was to reveal His faithfulness and restore Job in greater measure.

As we face trials on our own journey, let us emulate Job's endurance and unwavering faith. Trust in God's sovereignty, knowing that He sees our circumstances and remains faithful. Seek the guidance of the Holy Spirit, who will empower and lead us through every challenge, enabling us to pass our tests and come out stronger on the other side.

Satan made a powerful statement, questioning Job's faith and suggesting that Job's devotion to God was solely based on the blessings and protection he received. Satan insinuated that if Job were to lose everything, he would curse God. This highlights the reality that in our journey of faith, there is a spiritual battle taking place. Satan seeks to challenge and undermine our faith in God, while God trusts and believes in us to remain faithful in the face of trials.

Job's story exemplifies the protection and blessings that come from trusting and fearing God. God had placed a hedge of protection around Job, blessing his work and increasing his possessions. Job was a man of integrity and devotion to God, and Satan sought to prove that Job's faith was conditional and would crumble under adversity.

However, despite Satan's accusations, God allowed Satan to touch all that Job had, but he was not permitted to harm Job himself. Job endured great loss—his possessions, his children—but he did not curse God. Instead, he responded with humility, worship, and trust in God's sovereignty.

Job's journey teaches us important lessons about faith and trust in the midst of trials. It reveals the reality of spiritual warfare and the need to stand firm in our devotion to God, even when faced with intense suffering. It demonstrates that our faith is not dependent on external circumstances or blessings but on our trust in God's character and his redemptive plan.

As we navigate our own trials, we must remember that God trusts and believes in us to remain faithful. Satan may seek to challenge our faith, but we can draw strength from knowing that our Redeemer lives and that God's power and grace are sufficient to sustain us. Just as Job's story ultimately revealed God's faithfulness and restoration, may we trust in God's greater purpose and cling to our unwavering faith in Him. In Job's situation, Satan was given permission by God to touch everything Job had, except for his life. It is important to recognize that nothing can happen without God's knowledge and permission. The thief, referring to Satan, comes to steal, kill, and destroy, as stated in John 10:10. We can clearly see these destructive forces at work in Job's life.

Despite the immense suffering and loss, Job responded with an incredible act of worship. He tore his clothes, shaved his head, and bowed down before God. Even in the midst of deep pain and anguish, Job chose to worship God. He acknowledged that he came into the world with nothing and would leave with nothing, recognizing that all blessings and possessions come from the Lord.

Job's response demonstrates his unwavering trust and faith in God's sovereignty. He did not blame God or accuse Him of wrongdoing. Instead, Job praised and blessed the name of the Lord, acknowledging His authority and goodness. Job remained righteous and did not sin against God.

Job's example teaches us the importance of worshipping God, even in the midst of adversity. It reveals that worship is not contingent on our circumstances but is an expression of our reverence, trust, and faith in God. In times of trial and suffering, worship becomes even more significant, as it allows us to shift our focus from the pain to the greatness and faithfulness of our Creator.

The story of Paul and Silas in Acts 16 also illustrates the power of worship in challenging situations. Despite being imprisoned and facing severe circumstances, they prayed and sang hymns to God. Their worship not only impacted their own hearts but also caught the attention of the other prisoners.

In difficult times, it is natural to cry out and express our emotions. However, true worship goes beyond our immediate circumstances and focuses on the greatness and faithfulness of God. It allows us to find strength and hope in Him, even when everything around us seems to be falling apart.

May we learn from the examples of Job, Paul, and Silas and embrace a heart of worship, even in the midst of trials. Let us magnify the name of the Lord and find solace in His presence, knowing that He is worthy of our praise and trust, regardless of our circumstances.

Indeed, the story of Paul and Silas in Acts 16 continues with a powerful manifestation of God's power. As they were praying and singing hymns to God in prison, suddenly there was an earthquake that shook the foundations, opened the prison doors, and loosened everyone's chains. It was a miraculous deliverance.

This event demonstrates that even in the midst of suffering, persecution, and imprisonment, God has the power to intervene and bring about supernatural breakthroughs. Paul and Silas, despite being beaten, chained, and in a state of physical discomfort, trusted in God and praised Him. Their faith and worship unleashed God's power, resulting in their freedom and the liberation of others as well.

This serves as a reminder that, as followers of Christ, we may face various challenges, including persecution and suffering, for the sake of the Gospel. However, we are not to be fearful or ashamed. God has given us a spirit of power, love, and soundness of mind, as mentioned in 2 Timothy 1:7. With this empowering spirit, we can endure and overcome any trials we face, knowing that God's power is at work in us.

Satan's attempts to lead Job into sin were unsuccessful. However, he did not give up. He returned with different strategies to try to break Job's faith and trust in God. It is important for us to remain vigilant and stand firm against the schemes of the enemy. The journey of faith will inevitably involve spiritual battles, but we can find strength in the life of Jesus manifested in our mortal flesh, as mentioned in 2 Corinthians 4:11. Through our struggles and challenges, the life of Jesus is revealed, and His power sustains us.

As we encounter difficulties on our journey, let us remember that God's power is greater than any opposition we may face. Like Paul and Silas, let us worship and trust in Him, knowing that He can bring deliverance, breakthrough, and victory in even the most challenging circumstances.

13

TRIALS AND SPIRITUAL TRANSFORMATION

We all encounter various trials and challenges on our journey to the cross. When Satan suffers defeat and his plans fail, he returns with tactics that target our flesh. It is crucial to die to the flesh and resist the devil, for he will flee from us. Let us live according to the Spirit of God, as the flesh is weak while the Spirit is willing. This transformation from flesh to Spirit enables us to withstand Satan's attacks. In Job 2:4 (KJV), Satan responds to the Lord, stating, "Skin to skin, yea, all that a man hath, he will give for his life." Then Satan suggests, "But put forth thy hand now, and touch his bone and his flesh, and he will curse thee to thy face." The Lord allows Satan to afflict Job but spares his life. Consequently, Satan afflicts Job with severe boils from head to toe, with God's permission.

During these trials, Job's wife, who should have been his source of encouragement and support, fails him. Instead of standing with him, she tries to lead him into sinning against God. In Job 2:8 (KJV), his wife tells him, "Dost thou remain thine integrity?

Curse God and die." She aligns herself with Satan's desires, echoing his strategy from the Garden of Eden, hoping it will work once again. However, Job remains faithful to God and preserves his integrity. It is essential to guard our speech during times of trial, refraining from uttering words that disrespect our Heavenly Father. As Psalm 19:14 (KJV) states, "Let the words of my mouth and the meditation of my heart be acceptable in thy sight, O Lord, my strength and my redeemer."

When Job's trial comes to an end, God restores to him all that he lost a hundredfold. However, when Job's friends arrive, they tear their clothes and remain silent for seven days. At this point, Job's mind becomes consumed by negative thoughts, leading him to wrongly perceive himself. Job's friends begin to speak negatively about his situation, judging it based on their limited understanding, as if Job and his family had sinned against God. Along this journey, family, friends, and relatives may distance themselves due to the challenges. But let us not give up and instead trust in God's faithfulness. This process is part of the journey, as Joel 2:25 (KJV) assures, "I will restore to you the years that the locust hath eaten, the cankerworm, the caterpillar, and the palmerworm, my great army, which I sent among you." The difficult trial is followed by restoration, and we must remember that temptation is not a place where God sends us.

Temptation involves a confrontation between a person and the devil. In Luke 4:1 (KJV), Jesus, filled with the Holy Ghost, returns from Jordan and is led by the Spirit into the wilderness, where He is tempted by the devil for forty days. Jesus fasts during this time, and when it ends, He experiences hunger. Satan approaches Him, saying, "If thou be the Son of God, command this stone that it be made bread." Jesus responds, "It is written that man shall not live by bread alone, but by every word of God." Jesus wields the sword of the Spirit, which is the word of God, in his defense. Satan then takes Jesus to a high mountain and shows Him the kingdoms of the world in an instant. Satan offers Jesus all the power and glory if He would worship him. However, Jesus rebukes him, saying, "Get thee behind me, Satan; for it is written, Thou shalt worship the Lord thy God, and him only shalt thou serve." Despite knowing that Jesus possesses the Holy Ghost's power and created everything in heaven, earth, and the sea, Satan refuses to give up. We, too, must know the word of God and our identity in Christ as we navigate this journey.

The devil brings Jesus to Jerusalem and places Him on the pinnacle of the temple, tempting Him to cast Himself down, quoting scripture to justify His actions. But Jesus replies, "It is said, Thou shalt not tempt the Lord thy God." When the devil finishes tempting Jesus, he departs from Him, but only for a season. Jesus withstands the temptation and denies Satan an opportunity. He resists and fights back with the word of God. Although Satan tries to twist the word, Jesus, being the Word of God Himself, remains unswayed. Let us be filled with the Holy Spirit and saturated with the word of God so that when the devil attempts to touch us, the word of God flows out like water from a sponge.

14

LOVE YOUR JUDAS

Matthew 26:47 (KJV): And while He yet spoke, lo, Judas, one of the twelve, came, and with him a great multitude with swords and staves, from the chief priests and elders of the people. Now he betrayed Him and gave them a sign, saying, "Whosoever I shall kiss, that same is He; hold Him fast."

The Word of God highlights the phrase "one of the twelve" to help us understand that many times, those who attack us are the ones closest to us. They are the people who know our ministry, our breakthroughs, and our downfalls. Satan often attacks through those who act as our "Judas." They may be present to help us complete our journey.

John 18, verse 4 (KJV): Jesus, therefore, knowing all things that should come upon Him, went forth, and said unto them, "Whom seek ye?" They answered, "Jesus of Nazareth." Jesus said unto them, "I AM He." And Judas also, who betrayed Him, stood with them. As soon as He had said unto them, "I AM He," they went backwards and fell to the ground.

On this journey, you will face the enemy. Several times on your way to the cross, you will come face-to-face with your enemies. Tell them who you are in Christ Jesus. Stand your ground and use the Word of God, which is sharper than any double-edged sword. The Word of God is the sword of the Spirit. In this verse, we see Jesus Christ using the name of God with power and authority, standing His ground, and facing the enemy. Our Father, God, is the Great I AM.

Exodus 3 verse 14 (KJV): And God said unto Moses, "I AM THAT I AM." And He said, "Thus shalt thou say unto the children of Israel, 'I AM' hath sent me unto you." If you stand your ground, the enemy will fall to the ground under your feet. Matthew 26 verse 48-49 (KJV): Now he who betrayed Him gave them a sign, saying, "Whosoever I shall kiss, that same is He; hold Him fast." And forthwith he came to Jesus and said, "Hail, Master!" and kissed Him.

On this journey, Satan can use people who are very close to your heart to destroy you. They may be friends with whom you have shared dreams and visions, prayed together for the Kingdom of God, or close relatives with whom you sit at the table and eat together. It could even be a spouse whom you kiss every day and night and share a bed with as one. Stand your ground and fight, not against flesh and blood, but against the spirit behind the betrayer. Enter the battlefield with a full understanding of who you are in Christ and who you are fighting against.

Put on the full armour of God. You will appear to the enemy

covered from head to toe. Hallelujah!

Ephesians 6:10–13 (KJV): Finally, my brethren, be strong in the Lord, and in the power of His might. Put on the whole armour of God, that ye may be able to stand against the wiles of the devil. For we wrestle not against flesh and blood, but against principalities, against powers, against the rulers of the darkness of this world, against spiritual wickedness in high places. Wherefore take unto you the whole armour of God, that ye may be able to withstand in the evil day, and having done all, to stand.

Take your stand like Jesus, our King ("I AM He"). When you take your stand, the enemy will fall.

Matthew 26 verse 50 (KJV): And Jesus said unto him, "Friend, wherefore art thou come?" Then they came and laid hands on Jesus and took Him.

Jesus knew where Judas was coming from when he said, "Friend, where are you coming from?" It was a reminder of their relationship and that He still saw him as a friend, even though He knew what Judas had done. Jesus was with God at the beginning of creation. He was one with God, the Father, and the Holy Spirit. Everything was created through Him, by Him, and for Him. The plan for Him to come to earth and die was discussed in Heaven, with all the details revealed to the prophets. He knew that every prophecy must be fulfilled, including Judas' betrayal. He was the Lamb of God who was slain before the foundation of the earth. He told the disciples what would happen to Him. Remember, He is the Alpha and Omega.

15

BETRAYED BY MY BEST FRIEND

I would like to share the story of my personal betrayal, which revolves around a close friendship I had in South Africa. My best friend and I shared the same names and had a special way of greeting each other in Zulu, using the term "Bizo," meaning "my name." Our bond was incredibly strong, and she felt like a sister to me. I trusted her wholeheartedly and confided in her about all my problems. Little did I know, she would become my Judas.

At the time, I was engaged and eagerly planning my wedding. Naturally, I involved my best friend in the process, as she was someone I believed I could rely on and help in any way possible. I even lent her my clothes on multiple occasions to ensure she looked presentable when going out. Our friendship was built on trust and support.

However, unbeknownst to me, my best friend was dating my ex-husband behind my back. During a period when my husband and I were going through a rough patch and experiencing disagreements, I confided in her, not suspecting her ulterior motives. Unfortunately, by sharing my struggles, I unknowingly provided her with the ammunition to capitalize on my downfall and build her own empire.

During that time, I wasn't particularly religious or saved, but I still held a deep trust in God and relied on Him for guidance. I fervently prayed for the success of my upcoming wedding, despite the turmoil I was facing. Growing up in a Christian family instilled in me a strong faith, which I held onto tightly during this trying period.

This experience taught me a valuable lesson about the complexities of human relationships and the importance of discernment in choosing our confidants. It's a painful reminder that even those closest to us can sometimes betray our trust. Nonetheless, my faith in God remained unshaken, serving as a source of solace and strength during this challenging time.

As I reflect on this chapter of my life, I am reminded of the resilience of the human spirit and the power of forgiveness. While the betrayal hurt deeply, I chose to let go of the anger and resentment, allowing healing to take place within my heart. This story serves as a testament to my growth and determination to overcome adversity, all while remaining true to my faith and principles.

In my family, the influence of Christianity was deeply rooted. My grandmother, a devoted reader of the Bible, ensured that we attended church every Sunday. But it was my great-grandmother who truly embodied the essence of a prayer warrior. Living in a humble village, she dedicated herself to prayer, spending over four hours each night communing with God. Her prayers were all-encompassing, extending to every member of our family.

Despite the heartbreaking loss of ten out of the twelve children she bore, from her firstborn to the tenth, God spared my grandmother's life so that she could become the caretaker and guardian of future generations, including me. In her nightly prayers, my great-grandmother would specifically mention each of our names, interceding for our parents as well. With a list of fourteen grandchildren and countless great-grandchildren, some of whom I cannot even recall, her prayers were extensive.

The power and length of her prayers often overwhelmed me, and I would inevitably drift off to sleep while still on my knees. But the conclusion of her prayer was always signalled by a gentle but firm tap on my back, jolting me awake. In her heartfelt conversations with God, she would lay bare her soul, sharing every aspect of her life, even including her enemies and neighbours. Witnessing her devotion, I couldn't help but feel that a seed was being planted deep within my spirit.

The impact of my great-grandmother's unwavering faith continues to resonate within me. It serves as a reminder of the strength that can be found in connecting with a higher power and pouring out one's heart in prayer. Her example taught me the importance of interceding for others, even amidst personal trials and tribulations. The seeds of faith she sowed in our family continue to grow, shaping the way we approach challenges and navigate our spiritual journeys.

Looking back, I am grateful for the legacy of faith that has been passed down through generations. It has provided me with a solid foundation and a deep-rooted belief in the power of prayer. I carry her teachings with me, knowing that prayer has the ability to transform lives and bring comfort, guidance, and healing.

At the tender age of ten, I began to learn the art of prayer. It became my sanctuary, a place where I could pour out my heart to God, share my deepest desires, and even express my fears of the things I hoped would never come to pass. Throughout it all, God remained steadfast and faithful.

In the tradition of my ex-husband's family, it was customary for the bride-to-be to live with her in-laws for three months as a way for them to assess her suitability as a future spouse for their son. In our case, his parents resided in a different city, nestled within a small village. During my stay with them, unbeknownst to me, my best friend betrayed our friendship by sleeping with my fiancé and spending nights at his house.

Weekend after weekend, when he was expected to visit his parents, he failed to show up. Concern began to grip his family as they wondered about his whereabouts. This was the year 1982 when telephones were not yet commonplace in village households and communication was primarily conducted through telegrams.

Unknown to me, those three months were spent with my friend as his new romantic interest. Meanwhile, preparations for our wedding were already in full swing, with both my family and his eagerly purchasing items for the ceremony. Upon my return, whispers and rumours surrounded me, painting a vivid picture of the betrayal that had occurred. In my quest for truth, I confronted him, only to be met with defensiveness and offensive tactics, leading me to question the validity of the rumours and doubt my own instincts.

This chapter of my life stands as a painful reminder that trust can be shattered, even by those closest to us. It taught me the importance of discernment and the need to address matters head-on, rather than succumbing to manipulative tactics that cloud the truth. While the pain was immense, I refused to let it consume me entirely.

In moments of despair, my faith in God remained unwavering. Through prayer, I found solace, guidance, and the strength to navigate the tumultuous emotions that threatened to over-whelm me. I sought divine intervention, surrendering the situation into God's hands and trusting that He would provide clarity and healing in due time.

Although the road to recovery was arduous, I learned to rely on my faith as an anchor, enabling me to forgive and release the weight of the past. While the scars may remain, they serve as a reminder of the resilience of the human spirit and the transformative power of faith in times of betrayal.

Today, I stand as a testament to the triumph of the human spirit, holding onto the lessons learned and embracing the future with renewed hope and an unwavering belief in the goodness that still exists in the world.

16

MARRIAGE BETRAYAL: BROKEN TRUST

People were envious of our upcoming marriage, and I naively believed their words. Upon my return from a trip, a young boy, who was meant to deliver a note to my ex-husband as we were neighbours, mistakenly handed it to me instead. Opening the note, I discovered it was written by my closest friend, informing my ex-husband that she was three months pregnant. I was devastated, unsure of what course of action to take. With only three months remaining until the wedding, I was torn between cancelling the ceremony or proceeding with it. Overwhelmed by a mix of emotions—heartbreak, betrayal, anger, and confusion—I cried out in despair.

Desperate for answers, I went to my friend's house, only to find out that she had left, taking all her belongings with her. Seeking guidance, I approached her aunt, who had always been like an older sister to me. However, she denied any knowledge of the situation, leaving me suspicious that she was hiding something. I decided to wait for my ex-husband to return from work, seething with anger, as I pondered the sacrifices I had made for his family and the efforts I had put into establishing a respectable reputation for him.

Reflecting on Proverbs 18:22, which states, "He who finds a wife finds what is good and receives favour from the Lord," I questioned the validity of this wisdom in my current circumstances.

Upon his arrival, I immediately confronted him with the letter. Shockingly, he denied any involvement and accused my friend of having multiple boyfriends. He insisted that she should take responsibility and inform the actual father of her unborn child. This led to a heated conflict between us. My grandmother, sensing the turmoil, urged me to call off the wedding. Initially, she had reservations about his trustworthiness, but she didn't want to shatter my happiness. Despite the doubts, I chose to forgive him and proceeded with the wedding, partly driven by the desire to prove to my best friend that he had chosen me over her betrayal. Now she was left with a child who would grow up without a father. I hoped this would serve as a wake-up call for her, highlighting the consequences of her actions. However, my efforts were in vain, as my friend left the city and never returned.

Eighteen years had passed since I exchanged vows. At that time, I found myself working in the Surgical Ward of St. Augustine Hospital. It was there that I unexpectedly crossed paths with her again. As I attended to patients, she humbly pushed a food trolley, distributing lunches to those in need. As a unified nursing staff, we worked diligently together, ensuring that each patient received their meals. When she caught sight of me, she was taken aback. At that time, I had undergone a spiritual transformation, embracing my faith as a born-again Christian, brimming with the love of Jesus Christ. At that moment, all I felt was the unconditional love of God in my heart for her. Without hesitation, I rushed towards her, enveloping her in a warm embrace, accompanied by a radiant smile. I greeted her using our familiar nickname for each other, "Oh, my dear Bizo." While she appeared somewhat emotional, my overwhelming sentiment was the genuine love of God I had for her as my best friend—nothing more. I refrained from delving into the past, accepting her without any reference to our previous history.

Curious about her current employment, I inquired whether she was working full-time. She revealed that she was covering a shift for a colleague who had fallen ill. I assumed she had given birth to a daughter, but I lacked further details. I sensed that it was God's intention for me to encounter my "Peter" and reconcile with her. Regrettably, she eventually resigned from the hospital, departing from my life once again. My heart ached, as I had no intention of causing her any discomfort. From that point forward, I never had the opportunity to see her again. This experience taught me to love both my "Peter" and my "Judas" unconditionally.

Feeling a responsibility towards the child, I approached my ex-husband and inquired whether he had attempted to contact her and meet their potential daughter. I wanted him to be a part of the child's life if he was indeed the father. However, he evaded discussing the matter, remarking that the girl bore a resemblance to his older sister. It's important to note that this incident did not directly contribute to the breakdown of my marriage. The extramarital relationships and resulting children born outside of our marriage were ongoing issues that preceded this particular incident.

In 2 Corinthians 10:3−4, it is revealed that although we live in the physical realm, our battles are not fought with mere physical means. Our weapons are mighty before God, capable of tearing down strongholds, dispelling imaginations, and toppling everything that exalts itself against the knowledge of God. These weapons bring every thought into captivity, obedient to Christ. When faced with approaching storms, what weapon should one employ?

The arsenal bestowed upon us consists of the Blood of Jesus Christ, the Word of God, the Name of Jesus, and prayer. Hebrews 4:12 describes the Word of God as quick, powerful, and sharper than any double-edged sword. It pierces deeply, discerning the thoughts and intents of the heart. The Word of God is an extraordinary weapon, entrusted to us, to combat our enemies. In fact, Jesus Himself employed the Word of God to resist the devil. In Luke 4:2−8, He brandished the sword of the Spirit, which is the Word of God, confidently declaring, "It is written."

Therefore, when faced with adversity and impending storms, we must equip ourselves with the Word of God, allowing it to be our sword and shield. Through the power of God's Word, we have the ability to overcome and conquer any challenge that comes our way.

17

RECEIVING SALVATION

S alvation cannot be achieved without the shedding of Christ's blood. We must also undergo a spiritual death in our own flesh. Matthew 26:66 reflects this truth when it says, "What do you think?" They answered, "He is guilty of death." Throughout history, we have witnessed the persecution, torture, and imprisonment of God's children for their faith in Christ. Just as Christ was sentenced to death, believers today face death sentences in various parts of the world for standing firm in the truth of our Savior. Christian persecution continues to occur even in present times. Jesus Himself foretold that the world would treat us as it treated Him. 2 Corinthians 4 verse 8 encapsulates our experiences: "We are hard-pressed on every side, yet not crushed; we are perplexed, but not in despair; persecuted, but not forsaken; struck down, but not destroyed." In our mortal bodies, we carry the dying of the Lord Jesus so that His life may be revealed through us. Paul's words to the Corinthians make it clear that troubles, persecutions, and even death are inevitable on this journey for the sake of Christ.

Our own experiences of death and persecution serve to crucify our flesh, allowing the full manifestation of Jesus Christ to be seen in our lives. Jesus died on the Cross to give us new life, and we too must die to our flesh in order to receive this new life in Christ. John 12:24 emphasizes this truth: "Most assuredly, I say to you, unless a grain of wheat falls into the ground and dies, it remains alone; but if it dies, it produces much grain." Through His death, Jesus Christ granted us new life and became the seed that died, yielding an abundant harvest. Our salvation is not merely for ourselves; it is a call to bring people into the Kingdom of God, which requires us to completely die to ourselves and experience the fullness of His glory. Matthew 26:67 recounts the abuse Jesus endured: "Then they spat in His face and beat Him; and others struck Him with the palms of their hands, saying, 'Prophesy to us, Christ! Who is the one who struck You?'" Similarly, those who evangelize and proclaim salvation today may face ridicule, physical violence, and even death. This is the path we must tread.

Romans 8:18 (KJV) states, "For I consider that the sufferings of this present time are not worthy to be compared with the glory which shall be revealed in us." Likewise, 2 Corinthians 1:5 (KJV) affirms, "For as the sufferings of Christ abound in us, so our consolation also abounds through Christ." In Luke 21:12, Jesus warned that believers would be persecuted, handed over to authorities, and imprisoned for the sake of His name. The words spoken by Jesus will never return empty; they will accomplish what He declared. The testing of our faith and our gifts will come. Doubts may arise, questioning our calling as prophets or leaders of ministries. We may wonder why God did not reveal forthcoming problems so we could pray against them in our prophetic capacity.

During seasons of spiritual recession, transition, and upheaval, people may question your faith—perhaps even those who have stood by your side throughout the journey. In such moments, follow the example of Jesus Christ and maintain your composure, commanding your flesh to die. The Spirit of God will raise a standard for you. Moses, the prophet of God, faced similar challenges with his brother Aaron and sister Miriam, as recounted in Numbers 12 verses 1–2. "Then Miriam and Aaron spoke against Moses because of the Ethiopian woman whom he had married; for he had married an Ethiopian woman. So they said, 'Has the Lord indeed spoken only through Moses? Has He not spoken through us also?' And the Lord heard it." Moses was also on a journey, enduring trials and tribulations.

18

DIVINE REVELATION

T he scribes consistently opposed the teachings of Jesus Christ, manipulating the law to resist Him. Unbeknownst to them, Christ Himself is the embodiment of the Word of God. He is the very essence that the law speaks of, being its author. Every aspect of the law pointed to Him—the first-born lamb without defect, the manna from heaven, and even Jacob's vision of the ladder connecting heaven and earth. It was all a representation of Him.

In Matthew 23:13–16, Jesus pronounced woe upon the scribes and Pharisees, denouncing their hypocrisy. They closed off the kingdom of heaven to others while refusing to enter themselves. They exploited widows, pretending to be devout with lengthy prayers, and their condemnation would be severe. They traversed land and sea to make converts, but they only succeeded in creating individuals even more misguided and corrupted than themselves.

These scathing words were spoken by our Lord Jesus Christ,

aimed at the scribes and Pharisees, who feigned righteousness but lacked true goodness within them.

The elders within the church are individuals appointed to fulfill various pastoral responsibilities, including preaching and serving the congregation. However, it is essential to recognize that if these appointments are made by human judgment rather than by God's guidance, conflicts and divisions can arise. Such appointments based on long service or financial support can be detrimental.

Throughout your journey, you may encounter persecution and trials that lead you to authorities who may pass judgment on you for the sake of Christ. The Lord Jesus Christ fearlessly spoke the truth to the scribes, exposing their actions that hindered people from understanding the truth. His words were direct and unwavering. As you embark on this journey, it is crucial to consistently proclaim the truth, which is the Word of God. The truth has the power to set people free.

In 2 Timothy 3:16 (KJV), it is stated that all Scripture is inspired by God and serves a purpose in doctrine, reproof, correction, and instruction in righteousness. Through these Scriptures, the person of God can be thoroughly equipped for every good work. This provision serves as a guide on the journey towards the cross, ensuring one's preparedness for all endeavours.

It is vital to uphold the truth, follow the path set by God, and rely on His Word throughout your journey.

As followers of Christ, we are called to be the salt of the earth, testifying to His goodness and spreading His message. In Matthew 26:61, false witnesses accused Jesus, claiming that He had spoken about destroying and rebuilding the temple of God in three days. The high priest questioned Him, asking if He had anything to say in response. However, Jesus chose to remain silent. This teaches us the importance of not opening the door to provocation, just as Jesus held His peace.

We must remember Philippians 4:7, which assures us that the peace of God, surpassing all understanding, will guard our hearts and minds through Christ Jesus. Instead of engaging in arguments with our enemies, we should hold on to the peace of God and overcome. Jesus exemplified this when the high priest asked Him directly if He was the Christ, the Son of God, in Matthew 26:63. Jesus acknowledged the truth of who He was, stating that the high priest would witness Him sitting on the right hand of power and coming in the clouds of heaven. This response led the high priest to accuse Him of blasphemy. However, Jesus spoke the truth, even though it was hidden from the worldly wise.

In our own lives, we should hold steadfast to the truth and not be swayed by the opinions or accusations of others. Just as Jesus could not deny who He was and is to come, we too should boldly proclaim the truth of Christ, even when it may be misunderstood or rejected by the world.

The truth of who Jesus was requires divine revelation. Not everyone, including the disciples, fully understood His identity except for Peter, son of Jonah, who received the revelation from God the Father. To the high priest and others, Jesus appeared to be a mere man, the son of Joseph. However, Jesus was and is the Son of God, destined to sit at the right hand of God in heaven. He had a clear understanding of His purpose and destination.

In 1 Corinthians 2:7-8, it is stated that the wisdom of God is spoken in a mystery, a hidden wisdom that God ordained before the world for our glory. This wisdom was unknown to the rulers of this world, for had they known, they would not have crucified the Lord of Glory. It was through His crucifixion that Jesus accomplished our salvation. He had to die for our sins.

The mystery of God's plan and the revelation of Jesus' identity were not readily apparent to all. It took the working of God's wisdom and divine intervention for individuals to grasp the truth. Jesus' death on the cross was a necessary sacrifice that saved us from the consequences of our sins.

As believers, we can acknowledge and appreciate the depth of God's wisdom and the profound significance of Jesus' sacrifice on our behalf. Through His death and resurrection, we find redemption and eternal life.

19

TRUSTING THE LORD'S GUIDANCE

Although it may be difficult to contemplate, there is no salvation without the sacrificial shedding of Christ's blood. We, too, must die to our fleshly desires. In Matthew 26:66, when asked their thoughts, the response was that Jesus was guilty of death. We have witnessed the children of God being persecuted, tortured, and imprisoned for the sake of the gospel. Similarly, in various countries, Christians continue to face persecution even today. As Jesus foretold, what was done to Him will be done to us.

In 2 Corinthians 4:8, Paul wrote about being troubled on every side yet not distressed, perplexed but not in despair, persecuted but not forsaken, cast down but not destroyed. He emphasized that, as believers, we carry in our bodies the dying of the Lord Jesus so that His life might be manifested in us. Paul made it clear that troubles, persecutions, and even death would be part of the journey for the sake of Christ.

Our own suffering and persecution serve to crucify our flesh, allowing the full manifestation of Jesus Christ in our lives. Jesus' death on the cross granted us new life, but we must also die to our flesh to fully receive this new life in Christ. In John 12:24, Jesus likened Himself to a seed that must fall to the ground and die to bear abundant fruit. His death brought forth the first fruits, and in the same way, our salvation calls us to bring people into the kingdom of God at the cost of dying completely to ourselves and experiencing the fullness of His glory.

In Matthew 26:67, it is described how Jesus was spat on, beaten, and mocked. Similarly, some children of God who evangelize and proclaim salvation face persecution, physical abuse, and even death. This is the reality of the journey.

Romans 8:18 states that the sufferings of this present time are not worthy to be compared with the glory that will be revealed in us. And in 2 Corinthians 1:5, it is noted that as the sufferings of Christ abound in us, so does our consolation. Luke 21:12 warns that believers will face persecution and be delivered up to authorities for the sake of Christ's name.

During times of recession, transition, and challenges in the spiritual realm, people may question your faith, including those who were once supportive. In such moments, like Jesus, hold your peace and command your flesh to die. The Spirit of God will raise a standard for you. Similar situations occurred with Moses, Aaron, and Miriam in Numbers 12:1–2, when they spoke against Moses for marrying an Ethiopian woman and questioned if God only spoke through him. Yet, Moses continued on his journey.

In the face of trials and persecution, remember that the word spoken by Jesus will not return void but will accomplish its purpose. The testing of faith and gifts will come, but through it all, hold firm, trusting in the Lord's guidance and His ultimate plan.

20

DEALING WITH OFFENSE

A ccording to Matthew 26:69 (KJV), Now Peter sat outside in the palace, and a servant girl came to him, saying, "You also were with Jesus of Galilee." But he denied it before them all, saying, "I do not know what you are talking about." And when he had gone out to the gateway, another girl saw him and said to those who were there, "This fellow also was with Jesus of Nazareth." And again, he denied with an oath, "I do not know the man." Peter denied Christ three times and even swore that he did not know Him. Verse 74: Then he began to curse and swear, saying, "I do not know the man!" And immediately the rooster crowed. This is the man who said he would die where Jesus died. This is the man who received revelation from God about who Jesus was and is. This is the man whose name was changed from Simon to Peter because of the revelation. He remembered what the Lord said at the Last Supper. He went away and wept bitterly.

On your journey, you will encounter people like Peter. They will stand by your side when things are going well. They will be closer to you than a brother. They will promise to support you and help you through difficult times. But when the storms and challenges of this world come upon you, they will slowly distance themselves from you to see if you can overcome the storm. Day by day, they will move further away until they disappear. If others ask them if they were part of your ministry, they will deny it because they do not want to be associated with your struggles and failures. They only want to be counted among your successes, as if they played a crucial role in your elevation to where God has placed you.

Love your "Peters" because they teach you to trust in God alone and not rely on human strength. Matthew 27 verse 1 (KJV): When morning came, all the chief priests and elders of the people took counsel against Jesus and put Him to death. And when they had found Him, they led Him away and delivered Him to Pontius Pilate, the governor. This is the path to the cross. The chief priest is the person appointed by God to serve in the temple and guide people according to God's will. He knows the law and has witnessed the Lord preaching, teaching, healing the sick, performing miracles, and setting captives free. The chief priests in our present time are those who hold prominent positions: leaders, seniors, and elders who are ordained to serve God and the people in the church. God has bestowed different gifts of the Holy Spirit upon us to serve in unity and edify the body of Christ, the church. Our purpose is not to compete with one another but to work cooperatively, with one accord, and in unity. However, if one or two individuals who are not in prominent positions happen to be used by God in a special way, with the anointing flowing and the abundance of God's glory and love manifesting through them, the spirit of the chief priest may rise up and attempt to silence them.

The chief priests do not want anyone to operate with gifts or abilities that they themselves cannot possess. They believe that God should only speak to them and that they should be at the forefront. Instead of cherishing and praying for more people to receive the anointing, they become your enemies. It is important to remember that the gifts we receive are from God, and we should not boast about them. The chief priests will criticize everything you do and even try to turn people against you. This is the same reason why they handed Jesus over to the governor instead of protecting Him. His ministry, filled with power, wisdom, love, grace, and mercy, was difficult for them to understand. They felt threatened by Him. Do not be discouraged. Love them and pray for them.

Matthew 10:17 (KJV) warns us to be cautious of people who will deliver us to councils and persecute us in their synagogues. You may be brought before governors and kings to testify about your faith to them and the Gentiles. This is part of our journey; otherwise, Jesus Christ would not have mentioned it.

Matthew 27:3 (KJV) tells us about Judas, who betrayed Jesus. When he realized that Jesus was condemned, he repented and returned the thirty pieces of silver to the chief priests and elders, confessing his sin of betraying innocent blood. However, they dismissed him, saying it was his responsibility. There is a time for everything. Some people who turn against you may feel convicted in their souls but may not be able to undo the damage they caused. It is important to forgive them and show them love. Do not repay evil with evil. Remember that God is a righteous judge.

Romans 12:20 – 21 (KJV) teaches us that if our enemy is hungry, we should feed them; if they are thirsty, we should give them something to drink. By doing this, we heap coals of fire on their heads. We should not be overcome by evil, but overcome evil with good. Romans 12 verse 14 (KJV) encourages us to bless those who persecute us and not to curse them. This is the way Jesus taught us to deal with offences in our hearts and with offenders.

Matthew 27:11 (KJV) describes Jesus standing before the governor, who asked Him if He was the King of the Jews. Jesus replied, "You said it." In this journey, expect people to question your faith, especially when you are going through difficult times. Some will mock you because of your faith in Jesus Christ and the challenges you face. It is part of the journey. It is not easy, but hold on to Jesus, His Word, His promises, and His grace. Matthew 24:9 (KJV) states that many will be offended, betray one another, and hate one another. This is the time when we need more grace to overcome hatred with love.

Matthew 27:12 (KJV) mentions that when Jesus was accused by the chief priests and elders, He remained silent and did not answer. It is important to keep your peace in front of accusers.

Matthew 27 verses 14-15 (KJV) tells us that Pilate asked Jesus if He heard all the accusations made against Him, but Jesus did not respond. The governor marvelled at His silence. In this journey, learn not to open your mouth and try to defend yourself when people rise against you. Let God fight for you. Defend who you are in Christ, not what you have done. That is what

Jesus did. When asked if He was the King of the Jews, He simply replied, "You said it." When accused of what He said and did, He remained silent or quoted the Word of God.

2 Chronicles 20:15 (KJV) states, "Do not be afraid or dismayed because of this great multitude, for the battle is not yours, but God's." Do not try to justify yourself because the Lord God Almighty will justify you. Romans 8:30 (KJV) says that whom He predestined, He also called, and whom He called, He also justified. Jesus, the Son of God, was baptized by John the Baptist, and we witnessed the manifestation of the Trinity of God. Luke 3:16 (KJV) describes how the Spirit of God descended upon Jesus like a dove, and a voice from heaven declared Him the beloved Son of God. God justifies His Son, and the Holy Spirit agrees. We do not need to argue with our enemies or try to prove them wrong. Let God fight on our behalf. If you know who you are in Christ, hold your peace.

Matthew 27:15 (KJV) mentions that during a feast, the governor intended to release a prisoner chosen by the people. They had a notable prisoner named Barabbas. Pilate thought they would release Jesus and keep Barabbas imprisoned for his crimes, but they did the opposite. Jesus had already taken upon Himself the sins of Barabbas so that he could be set free and live. We can see the exchange of life there. Hallelujah! Jesus, the Son of Man, could take upon Himself everything you have ever done and set you free. Isaiah 61 verse 1 (KJV) states that the Spirit of the Lord God is upon Him to preach good tidings, bind up the brokenhearted, proclaim liberty to the captives, and open the prison to those who are bound.

Matthew 27:26 (KJV) describes how Jesus was scourged and handed over to be crucified after they mocked Him. People may devalue you and bring shame and disgrace upon you, but remember that Jesus faced the same afflictions and overcame the world. Revelation 12:11 declares that we overcome the enemy by the blood of the Lamb and the word of our testimony.

Matthew 27:29 (KJV) mentions how they placed a crown of thorns on Jesus' head and a reed in His right hand. They mocked Him, calling Him the King of the Jews. While they thought they were mocking Him, they were actually acknowledging His kingship. They bowed down before the King of Kings, even though they gave Him a reed, symbolizing weak rulership. If their eyes were opened, they would have seen Jesus at the right hand of the Father in heaven, wearing a crown of glory and power. Matthew 5:11 teaches that we are blessed when people insult, persecute, and falsely say evil things about us because of Jesus. Mocking is part of our journey.

Jesus endured it all. 2 Peter 3:3−4 warns us that scoffers will arise in the last days, following their own sinful desires and questioning the promise of Jesus' return. As children of God, we will face persecution and trouble. 2 Corinthians 4, verse 8, reminds us that although we may experience troubles on every side, we are not defeated. We may not know what to do, but we do not give up. We continually experience the death of Jesus in our own bodies. Proverbs 19:11 tells us that wisdom leads to patience, and it is to our glory to overlook an offense. Proverbs 29:11 states that a fool gives full vent to their anger, but a wise person quietly holds it in. Jesus did not answer Pilate's questions or the accusations made against Him by the multitudes. He held

His peace. Learn not to answer every inappropriate question and not to justify yourself. Allow God to justify you.

Matthew 27:31 mentions that after mocking Jesus, they took off the robe and led Him away to be crucified. People may devalue and shame you, but remember that Jesus faced the same affliction. And He overcame the world. Revelation 12:11 states that we overcome the enemy by the blood of the Lamb and the word of our testimony. Matthew 27:32 describes how they found a man from Cyrene named Simon and compelled him to bear the cross. During the hardships of your journey, God will raise someone to help you. He will never leave you or forsake you.

21

DYING WITH CHRIST

During the season you are in, God will appoint specific individuals to serve a unique purpose. However, it's crucial to remember that their role is temporary. Matthew 27:34 states that they gave Jesus vinegar mixed with gall to drink. In this journey, patience, perseverance, and long-suffering play significant roles as they are fruits of the Spirit. Matthew 27:35 (KJV) tells us that they crucified Him and divided His garments by casting lots, fulfilling the prophecy that said, "They divided My garments among them, and for My clothing they cast lots." People may gamble with your life, but be cautious and do not be discouraged or dismayed.

Matthew 27:37 states that they placed a sign above Jesus' head with the accusation, "THIS IS JESUS THE KING OF THE JEWS." Everything they did, thinking it was mockery, actually spoke the truth. He died as the King of the Jews and our King, the King of Kings and Lord of Lords. Though they bowed down in mockery, they inadvertently demonstrated respect and exaltation both prophetically and in real life.

Matthew 27:38 mentions that two thieves were crucified with Jesus, one on His right hand and another on His left. The fact that the King was not alone confirmed His kingship in both His death and as the King of Kings. God will bring confusion into the enemy's camp. People may indirectly elevate you while secretly planning to pull you down. Genesis 50, verse 20, reminds us that what others meant for evil, God can turn into good. Do not fear or be dismayed; trust in God. He will deliver you.

Matthew 27:40 (KJV) records people mocking Jesus, saying, "If You are the Son of God, come down from the cross." People will mock us as well, pointing out our challenges and problems and questioning our faith. They may ask, "If you are a real Christian, why are you going through these situations? Why are your children struggling with addiction despite you being a pastor?" Do not answer them, but hold your peace. Do not be discouraged by such questions or doubt God's help.

Matthew 27:41 (KJV) describes the chief priests, scribes, and elders mocking Jesus, saying, "He saved others, but He cannot save Himself! If He is the King of Israel, let Him come down from the cross, and we will believe Him." Beware of scribes and Pharisees on your journey. They can be found within the church and often use questions like "why" and "if." Luke 5 verses 21, 30, and 33 (KJV) highlight how the scribes and Pharisees questioned and criticized Jesus, questioning His authority to forgive sins and finding fault in His associations. Do not reject them, but stand on the truth and correct them with love and gracious words.

The scribes and Pharisees are often present to find faults in other children of God. Instead of contributing to positive change, they complain and murmur when others try to do good things for Christ. Their job is to accuse others. Do not be discouraged by their actions, but stay firm in the truth, correcting them with love and grace.

Matthew 27:46 portrays Jesus crying out with a loud voice, saying, "My God, My God, why have You forsaken Me?" There may be times in our lives when we feel as though God is no longer with us. These are the winter seasons when everything appears dry and we feel separated from God. However, God is always with us. He allows certain things to happen for a greater purpose, to reveal His glory through our circumstances. God separated Himself from His Son to allow death to take place. If the Son of God had been one with the Father, death would have had no power. Yet, in that separation, God's plan was fulfilled.

Jesus did not say, "My Father, My Father, why have You forsaken Me?" Instead, He addressed God. Deuteronomy 31:8 assures us that the Lord goes before us, and He will never leave us nor forsake us. Joshua 1:9 commands us to be strong and courageous, not to fear or be dismayed, for the Lord is with us wherever we go. In times of difficulty, we may feel separated from God, but He is still with us, working out His plan in our lives.

Matthew 27:47 (KJV) mentions that some of the bystanders thought Jesus was calling for Elijah. Misunderstandings can lead to the wrong conclusions. Jesus was not calling for Elijah; He was calling out to God, His Father.

During your journey, people may not understand the path you're on, even fellow believers, but God understands everything. Jeremiah 33 verse 3 (KJV) encourages us to call upon Him, and He will answer, revealing mighty things we do not know. Psalm 91 verse 15 (KJV) assures us that when we call upon God, He will answer and be with us in trouble, delivering us. Call upon Him first, rather than relying on people. Your fear may tell you to call the pastor, but first call upon God and then share your testimony with the pastor.

Matthew 27:48 depicts someone running to get a sponge, filling it with vinegar, and putting it on a reed to give Jesus something to drink. On this journey, there will be prophetic words spoken that must be fulfilled. Every word that comes from God's mouth will never return void but will accomplish its purpose. Jeremiah 29:11–12 (KJV) assures us that God has good plans for us, plans of peace and not evil, to give us a future and hope. When we call upon Him, He will listen. Psalm 69, verse 21 (KJV) prophesies about Jesus being given gall and vinegar to drink. David spoke of this while he was still in heaven as a spirit, before coming down to earth in human form. The prophecy was fulfilled, and the words were accomplished.

Matthew 27:49 (KJV) reveals that some bystanders said, "Let us see whether Elijah will come to save Him." There can be misunderstandings and misplaced expectations. The Lord Jesus Christ was in the final stage of fulfilling the Father's will. His cry confused the enemy, and the disciples were not present to support Him; they were hiding to save their own lives. However, they were still part of the Cross, as are we. Jesus became us on the Cross, standing in alignment with the Father's will. God's will may require sacrificing everything we are and have for His glory to manifest. Luke 9:23 reminds us that to follow Jesus, we must deny ourselves, take up our cross daily, and follow Him.

Why did Jesus mention the cross? What does the cross represent? He carried the Cross and followed the Father's will, dying to redeem us. John 12:24 (KJV) states that unless a grain of wheat falls into the ground and dies, it remains alone; but if it dies, it produces much fruit. Matthew 7:13–14 (KJV) describes the narrow path that leads to life, while the wide and broad path leads to destruction. We must die with Christ and crucify our flesh. May the grace of the Lord Jesus Christ be with you as you read this, and may the power of the Holy Spirit overshadow you. May your eyes be opened in Jesus' mighty name, and may deliverance and healing take place.

Thank you, Holy Spirit.

Printed in Great Britain
by Amazon